# Eastern
# Great Lakes

INDIANA ★ MICHIGAN ★ OHIO

*By*

Thomas G. Aylesworth
Virginia L. Aylesworth

CHELSEA HOUSE PUBLISHERS
New York          Philadelphia

**Produced by James Charlton Associates**
New York, New York.

Copyright © 1991 by Chelsea House Publishers, a division of Main Line Book Co.
All rights reserved. Printed and bound in the United States of America.

First Printing

1    3    5    7    9    8    6    4    2

**Library of Congress Cataloging-in-Publication Data**

Aylesworth, Thomas G.
    Eastern Great Lakes: Indiana, Michigan, Ohio/by
Thomas G. Aylesworth, Virginia L. Aylesworth.
    p.  cm. — (State reports)
    Includes bibliographical references and index.
    Summary: Discusses the geographical, historical, and cultural aspects of
Ohio, Indiana and Michigan
    ISBN 0-7910-1045-7
        0-7910-1392-8 (pbk.)
    1. Lake States—Juvenile literature. 2. Ohio—Juvenile States. 3. Indiana—Juvenile literature.
4. Michigan—Juvenile literature. [1. Lake States. 2. Ohio. 3. Indiana. 4. Michigan.] I. Aylesworth,
Virginia L. II. Title. III. Series: Aylesworth, Thomas G. State reports.

F551.A95    1991                          90-28842
977—dc20                                  CIP
                                          AC

# Contents

## Indiana

## Michigan

## Ohio

# Indiana

The Indiana seal, officially adopted in 1963, has evolved from the original territorial seal designed in 1801. It is circular, and shows two trees in the left background and three hills in the center background, with the sun shining between the first and second hill from the left. On the right are two sycamore trees. In the foreground are a woodsman with an ax and a buffalo jumping over a log. Surrounding the circle is "Seal of the State of Indiana" and at the bottom, the date 1816.

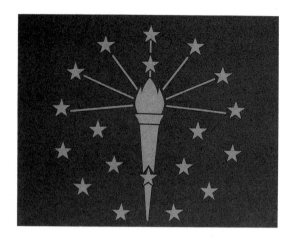

### State Flag

The Indiana state flag, designed by Paul Hadley of Mooresville, was adopted in 1917. The background is blue, and in the center is a torch symbolizing freedom and knowledge. Around the flaming torch are eighteen stars in gold. Above the flame is a nineteenth star, larger than the others, symbolizing Indiana's place as the nineteenth state. Above that is the word *Indiana.* On the handle of the torch is another star.

*Indiana's racing tradition moves from the speedway to the water at the Regatta and Governor's Cup Race in Madison.*

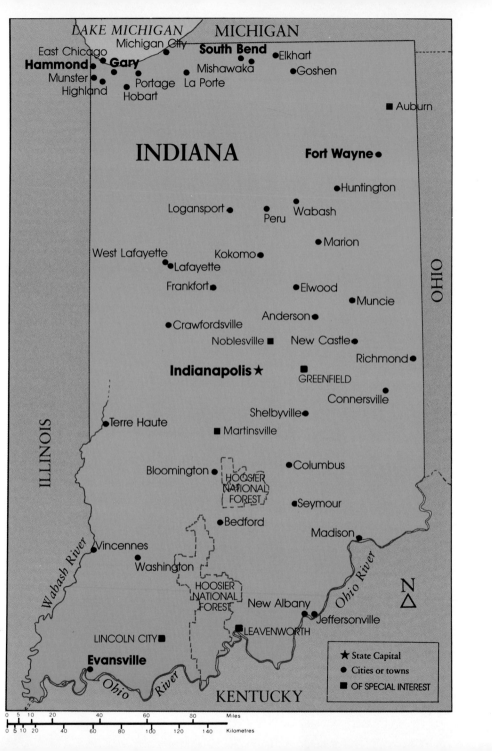

LAKE MICHIGAN  MICHIGAN

Michigan City
East Chicago
**South Bend**  Elkhart
**Hammond**  **Gary**  Mishawaka  Goshen
Munster  Portage  La Porte
Highland  Hobart

Auburn

**INDIANA**  **Fort Wayne**

Huntington

Logansport  Wabash
Peru

Marion

West Lafayette  Kokomo
Lafayette
Frankfort  Elwood
Muncie

Crawfordsville  Anderson
Noblesville  New Castle
Richmond

**Indianapolis** ★
GREENFIELD

Connersville

Terre Haute  Shelbyville
Martinsville

Bloomington  Columbus
HOOSIER
NATIONAL
FOREST
Seymour

Bedford
Madison
Vincennes
Washington

HOOSIER
NATIONAL
FOREST
New Albany
Jeffersonville
LINCOLN CITY  LEAVENWORTH

**Evansville**

Ohio  River

KENTUCKY

ILLINOIS

OHIO

Wabash River

Ohio River

N
△

★ State Capital
● Cities or towns
■ OF SPECIAL INTEREST

0  5  10    20        40        60        80      Miles
0  5 10   20     40      60      80    100   120   140   Kilometres

*The capitol building in Indianapolis.*

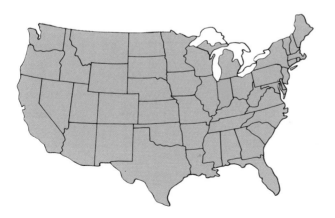

**State Capital**

Before statehood, the Indiana Territory had its capital in Vincennes (1800-13), and Corydon (1813-16). When Indiana became a state, Corydon remained the capital from 1816 to 1824. Indianapolis was named the capital in 1824. The first statehouse was built in 1835, but proved to be too small. The present capitol building, designed by Edwin May, was begun in 1878 and completed in 1888 at a cost of about $2 million. Built of Indiana limestone, it is four stories high and is topped by a golden dome, which reaches a height of 234 feet.

**State Motto**

*The Crossroads of America*

In 1937, the legislature created this motto. At the time, the center of the United States was in Indiana, and many north-south and east-west roads crossed in the state.

**State Name and Nicknames**

Indiana was named by the United States Congress when it created the Indiana Territory in 1800. The name simply means "Land of the Indians."

Officially, the nickname of Indiana is the *Crossroads of America,* as designated by the state legislature. But unofficially, it is most commonly referred to as the *Hoosier State.* No one seems to know the exact origin of the

*The state flower, the peony, is the fourth flower to be chosen since 1913.*

word "Hoosier," but there are several theories. Some say that a contractor, Samuel Hoosier, working on the Ohio Falls Canal at Louisville, Kentucky in 1826, gave employment preference to men living on the Indiana side of the Ohio River. These men became "Hoosier's Men." Others maintain that it stems from the early pioneers, who called out "Who's yare?" instead of "Who's there?" Still another explanation is that the word is a corruption of "husher," a word given to the early riverboat workers, who could hush anyone with brute force.

**State Flower**

The first state flower was adopted in 1913. From then on the state legislature kept changing its mind. At various times, the state flower was the carnation (family *Caryophyllus*), the flower of the tulip tree (*Liriodendron tulipfera*), and the zinnia (*Zinnia elegans*). In 1957, the

*The cardinal is Indiana's state bird.*

peony (*Paeonia*) was adopted, even though the flower is not native to the state.

**State Tree**

*Liriodendron tulipfera*, the tulip tree, was named the Indiana state tree in 1931. Other names for the tree are yellow poplar, blue poplar, hickory poplar, basswood, cucumber tree, tulipwood, whitewood, white poplar, and old-wife's-shirt tree.

**State Bird**

The cardinal, *Richmondena Cardinalis cardinalis*, or redbird, was adopted as the state bird in 1933.

### State Language

English has been the state language of Indiana since 1984.

### State Poem

In 1963, "Indiana," by Arthur Franklin Mapes, was named the state poem.

### State Stone

Limestone was designated the state stone in 1971.

### State Song

Selected in 1913, "On the Banks of the Wabash, Far Away," by Paul Dresser, is the state song.

### Population

The population of Indiana in 1990 was 5,564,228, making it the 14th most populous state. There are 153.7 persons per square mile, 64.2 percent of the population live in towns and cities. About 98 percent of the people in Indiana were born in the United States. Some 25 percent of the foreign-born came from Germany; other non-native groups include British, Canadians, Czechs, Hungarians, Italians, and Poles.

### Geography

Bounded on the north by Lake Michigan and the state of Michigan, on the east by Ohio and Kentucky, on the south by Kentucky, and on the west by Illinois, Indiana has an area of 36,185 square miles, making it the 38th largest state. The climate is temperate.

The highest point in the state, at 1,257 feet, is near Bethel in Wayne County. The lowest, at 320 feet, is in Posey County, near where the Wabash River flows into the Ohio River. In the south the state is hilly, in the central part it is a land of rolling plains, and in the north it is

*The scenic beauty of the Ohio River is equalled by its great history. Exhibits at the Ohio River Museum cover the early days of navigation and the age of steamboat travel.*

flat. The major waterways of the state are the Wabash, White, Tippecanoe, Eel, Mississinewa, Salamonie, St. Joseph, St. Marys, Maumee, Kankakee, Whitewater, and Ohio rivers. The largest lake is Lake Wawasee.

### Industries

The principal industries of Indiana are trade, agriculture, and services. The chief manufactured products are metals, transportation equipment, electrical and electronic equipment, non-electrical machinery, plastics, chemical products, and food products.

### Agriculture

The chief crops of the state are corn, sorghum, oats, wheat, rye, soybeans, and hay. Indiana is also a livestock state; and there are estimated to be some 1.2 million cattle, 4.4 million hogs and pigs, 82,757 sheep, and 28 million chickens on its farms. Oak, tulip, beech, and sycamore trees are cut.

Crushed stone, cement, gypsum, lime, sand, and gravel are important mineral resources. Commercial fishing brings in some $1.9 million a year.

### Government

The governor of Indiana is elected to a four-year term, as are the lieutenant governor, attorney general, secretary of state, auditor, treasurer, and superintendent of public instruction. All other elected state officers serve two-year terms. The state legislature, or general assembly, which meets annually, consists of a 50-member senate and a 100-member house of representatives. Legislators are elected from senatorial and house districts. Senators serve four-year terms, and representatives serve two-year terms. The most recent state constitution was adopted in 1851. In addition to its two U.S. senators, Indiana has ten representatives in the U.S.

House of Representatives. The state has twelve votes in the electoral college.

### History

Before Europeans arrived, what was to become Indiana was populated by prehistoric Indians called Mississippians. They were succeeded by Indians of the Miami tribe. Other tribes were to arrive in the area in the 1700s and 1800s. The Munsee and the Shawnee came in from the south, and the Huron, Kickapoo, Piankashaw, Potawatomi, and Wea came in from the north.

Probably the first European in the territory was the French explorer, Robert Cavelier, Sieur de la Salle, who arrived in 1679, traveling down the St. Joseph and Kankakee rivers. He came back in 1680 to explore part of the northern section. French fur traders from Canada followed, and in the 1720s, French fur-trading posts were built at Miami

*Historic Fort Wayne is a replica of the wooden fort for which the modern-day city of Fort Wayne was named. Guides dress as the original settlers did when the fort was built in 1815.*

(near today's Fort Wayne) and Ouiatenon (near what is now Lafayette). During the years 1731 and 1732, Indiana's first settlement was established by the French at Vincennes.

The British also began to trade with the Indians. After the French and Indian War, the English had title to the area. British troops occupied the territory during the Revolutionary War, moving into Vincennes. But in 1778, Virginia troops under George Rogers Clark captured the fort there. The British regained the fort, but once again Clark took it in 1779. That gave the United States control of the Northwest, and in 1787 Indiana became part of the Northwest Territory.

The Indiana Territory was created by the United States Congress in 1800, and it included what was to become Indiana, Illinois, and Wisconsin, plus parts of Michigan and Minnesota. The capital was in Vincennes, and William Henry Harrison was the first governor. By 1809, other territories in the area were set up, and Indiana had about the same boundaries it has today. That year, Harrison bought a large section of southern Indiana from the Indians. The Shawnee chief, Tecumseh, protested; several tribes, with weapons supplied by the British, banded together. They were beaten by Harrison in the Battle of Tippecanoe (near today's Lafayette) in 1811.

Indiana became the 19th state of the Union in 1816. By the 1850s, the state's economy was on the upswing. Railroads had been laid, farmers found new markets, and cities began to grow. Clement and Henry Studebaker opened their blacksmith and wagon shop in South Bend in 1852. It was later to become a prominent automobile concern. Richard Gatling invented the first machine gun in Indianapolis in 1862. James Oliver invented the hard-steel plow in the 1860s, and industry was on its way.

During the Civil War, although many Hoosiers joined the Union armed forces, there was only one battle fought on Indiana soil. In 1863, Confederate General John Hunt Morgan led his Raiders into Corydon, and later rode across eastern Indiana into Ohio.

After the war, industries developed rapidly. Natural gas was discovered near Portland in 1886. Huge oil refineries were built in Whiting in 1889. Elwood Haynes of Kokomo designed a successful gasoline-powered automobile in 1894. The Studebaker brothers began making electric automobiles in 1902. U.S. Steel began building the city of Gary in 1906.

During World War I, more than 130,000 Indianans served in the armed forces. During the 1920s the automobile and metal industries boomed. But Indiana, like most states, suffered during the Great Depression of the 1930s.

Then came World War II, when more than 340,000 Hoosiers joined the armed forces. After the war, more roads were built and

industry continued to expand. Today, the state continues to grow in industry, agriculture, and cultural affairs.

**Sports**

Many sporting events on the collegiate and secondary school level are scheduled all over the state. Indiana has always been known as the premier basketball state, and

*Basketball is the top sport in the state, and Notre Dame has produced many fine teams.*

the sport's popularity is referred to as "Hoosier Hysteria." For example, the state high school basketball tournament is not divided into classes; rather every high school in the state participates until a champion is crowned. Indeed, the first high school basketball championship game ever televised nationally was the 1989 Indiana final game.

On the collegiate level in basketball, Indiana University has won the NCAA national championship five times. In football, Purdue won the Rose bowl in 1967. The University of Notre Dame, a perennial football power, has made many post-season bowl appearances. On the professional level, the Indianapolis Colts of the National Football League play in the Hoosier Dome, and the Indiana Pacers of the National Basketball Association play in Market Square Arena in Indianapolis.

*Evansville's Old Vanderburgh County Courthouse, built in 1890, is now home to a theater group, a dance company, and art galleries.*

## Major Cities

*Evansville* (population 130,496). Founded in 1819, this Ohio River city has retained some of the atmosphere of the days when steamboats plied the waters of the river. It is the principal transportation, trade, and industrial center of southern Indiana.

*Things to see in Evansville:* Evansville Museum of Arts and Science, Reitz Home (1871), Wesselman Park, Angel Mounds State Historic Site, and Mesker Park Zoo.

*Fort Wayne* (population 172,028). Settled about 1690, Fort Wayne is located where the St. Joseph and St. Marys rivers join to form the Maumee River. Originally the headquarters of the Miami Indians, here the French established a fort in 1690. Fort Wayne became a major stop on the first railroad between Chicago and Pittsburgh in the 1850s, laying the foundation for the city's industrial development.

*Things to see in Fort Wayne:* Allen County-Fort Wayne Historical Society Museum, Louis A. Warren Lincoln Library and Museum, Fort Wayne Museum of Art, Historic Fort Wayne, Cathedral of the Immaculate Conception, Children's Zoo, Lakeside Rose Garden, and Foellinger-Freimann Botanical Conservatory.

*Tippecanoe Place in South Bend is near the site of the Battle of Tippecanoe, where William Henry Harrison's men fought Tecumseh's Shawnee warriors.*

Field Hall of Fame, State Library and Historical Building, Indiana State Museum, Morris-Butler House (1864), Indianapolis Museum of Art, Krannert Pavilion, Lilly Pavilion of Decorative Arts, Clowes Pavilion, Children's Museum, Eiteljorg Museum of the American Indian and Western Art, Patrick Henry Sullivan Museum, Muncie Art Center, Indianapolis Motor Speedway and Hall of Fame Museum, Hook's Historical Drug Store and Pharmacy Museum, Garfield Park, and Indianapolis Zoo.

**Indianapolis** (population 774,800). Founded in 1829, this city was a pastoral area of rolling woodlands when it was selected to be the new Indiana state capital. Chosen because it was at the geographical center of the state, the city was laid out in the wheel pattern of Washington, D.C. By the beginning of this century, it had developed into a manufacturing center. A cosmopolitan city, it has become the amateur sports capital of the United States.

*Things to see in Indianapolis:* State Capitol (1878-88), War Memorials Plaza, City Market, Union Station, President Benjamin Harrison Memorial Home (1874), Historic Lockerbie Square, James Whitcomb Riley Home, Scottish Rite Cathedral, Crown Hill Cemetery, Indiana Convention Center/Hoosier Dome, National track and

**South Bend** (population 109,727). Founded in 1823, the site was first visited by the explorers Father Marquette and Louis Jolliet between 1673 and 1675. But it was not until 1820 that a trading post was set up in the area. In 1823, Alexis Coquillard and Francis Comparet founded the town and began its industrial development. Today it is the industrial, cultural, and educational center of the north-central part of the state.

*Things to see in South Bend:*
Northern Indiana Historical Society Museum (1855), Council Oak Tree, Snite Museum of Art and O'Shaughnessy Hall Galleries, Church of the Sacred Heart (1871), Grotto of Our Lady of Lourdes, Century Center, Warner Gallery and Women's Art League gallery, The Studebaker National Museum, City Greenhouses and Conservatory, Rum Village, and East Race Waterway.

## Places to Visit

The National Park Service maintains four areas in the state of Indiana: Lincoln Boyhood National Memorial, Indiana Dunes National Lakeshore, George Rogers Clark National Historical Park, and Hoosier National Forest. In addition, there are 41 state recreation areas.

*Auburn*: Auburn-Cord-Duesenberg Museum. Three huge showrooms contain more than 140 antique cars, many of them illustrating Indiana's automotive past.

*Bloomington*: Thomas Hart Benton murals. Huge murals by the great painter can be seen in the Indiana University Auditorium.

*Columbus*: Architectural Tours. More than 50 public and business buildings designed by many world-famous architects can be seen in this small city.

*Connersville*: Whitewater Valley Railroad. Round-trip excursions can be taken on an early-1900s steam train.

*Elkhart*: Midwest Museum of American Art. This contains fine examples of the works of 19th- and 20th-century artists.

*French Lick*: House of Clocks Museum displaying a large collection of clocks, some of them dating back to the early 1800s.

*Jeffersonville*: Howard Steamboat Museum. Steamboat memorabilia are on exhibit in a 19th-century mansion.

*Lafayette*: Fort Ouiatenon. Reconstructions of the 1717 fort and trading post depict the history of the Wabash Valley.

*Martinsville*: Midwest Phonograph Museum. More than 600 antique record players and other memorabilia are on display.

*New Harmony*: Tour of Old Buildings. Many homes, stores, and other buildings from the early 19th-century.

*Noblesville*: Conner Prairie Settlement. A reconstruction of a prairie settlement of 1836.

*Peru*: Circus Museum. A vast collection of circus costumes and memorabilia.

*Richmond*: Levi Coffin House. This Federal-style brick house, built in 1839, was the home of a Quaker abolitionist who helped 2,000 fugitive slaves get to Canada.

*Rockville*: Historic Billie Creek Village. This is a recreation of a turn-of-the-century village and working farmstead.

*Terre Haute*: Eugene V. Debs home. This restored house was the home of the founder of the American Railway Union.

*Warsaw*: International Palace of Sports Hall of Fame. Displays wax figures of outstanding sports personalities.

*Wyandotte*: Wyandotte Cave. This limestone cavern is one of the world's largest.

## Events

There are many events and organizations that schedule activities of various kinds in the state of Indiana. Here are some of them:

*Sports*: Auto racing at International Dragway (Albany); Little 500 (Anderson); harness races and Free Fair (Anderson); Little 500 Bicycle Race (Bloomington); Whitewater Canoe Race (Connersville); Sugar Creek Canoe Race (Crawfordsville); GTE/US Men's Open Hardcourt Championships (Indianapolis); Indianapolis 500 Auto Race (Indianapolis); Regatta and Governor's Cup Race (Madison); Sprint Car races at Terre Haute Action Track (Terre Haute).

*Arts and Crafts*: antique car/art show (Aurora); Centerville Quilt Show (Centerville); Greentown Glass Festival (Kokomo); Midsummer Arts Festival (Lafayette).

*Music*: Indiana University Opera Theater (Bloomington); Ohio River Arts Festival (Evansville); Evansville Philharmonic (Evansville); Fort Wayne Philharmonic (Fort Wayne); Indianapolis Symphony (Indianapolis); Indianapolis Opera (Indianapolis); Footlight Musicals (Indianapolis); Starlight Musicals (Indianapolis); Fiddlers' Gathering (Lafayette); Marion Philharmonic (Marion); Lakefront Music Fest (Michigan City); South Bend Symphony (South Bend); Firefly Festival of the Performing Arts (South Bend).

*Entertainment*: Gaslight Festival (Anderson); Victorian Christmas (Aurora); Monroe County Fair (Bloomington); Madrigal Feasts (Bloomington); Harrison County Fair (Corydon); Germania Maennerchor Volkfest (Evansville); Germanfest (Fort Wayne); Three Rivers Festival (Fort Wayne); Johnny Appleseed Festival (Fort Wayne); Orange County Pumpkin Festival (French Lick); August Fest (Hammond); International Culture Festival (Hammond); Huntington County Heritage Days (Huntington); "500" Festival (Indianapolis); Indiana State Fair (Indianapolis); Steamboat Days Festival (Jeffersonville); Antique Steam Show (Lafayette); La Porte County Fair (La Porte); Iron Horse Festival (Logansport); Marion Easter Pageant (Marion); Michigan City Summer Festival (Michigan City); Summerfest (Mishawaka); Delaware County Fair (Muncie); Wine and Craft Festival (Nashville); Circus City Festival (Peru); Rose Festival (Richmond); Pioneer Day Festival (Richmond); Round

*The Indianapolis 500 is the largest one-day sporting event in the world; it draws about 400,000 spectators every year.*

Barn Festival (Rochester); Trail of Courage Rendezvous (Rochester); Civil War Days (Rockville); Parke County covered Bridge Festival (Rockville); "Thinking of Christmas" (Rockville); Rush County Fair (Rushville); Blue River Valley Pioneer Fair (Shelbyville); Maple Syrup Festival (South Bend); Ethnic Festival (South Bend); Sweet Sorghum Celebration (South Bend); Maple Sugarin' Days (Terre Haute); Wabash Valley Festival (Terre Haute); Spirit of Vincennes Rendezvous (Vincennes); Civil War Re-Enactment (Warsaw).

*Tours*: Gaslight Christmas (Anderson); Christmas Candlelight Tour (Crawfordsville); Candlelight Nights Tour (Madison); Log Cabin Tour (Nashville).

*Theater*: Shawnee Theater (Bloomfield); Embassy Theatre (Fort Wayne); Foellinger Theatre (Fort Wayne); Hilton U. Brown Theatre (Indianapolis); Indianapolis Civic Theater (Indianapolis); Indiana Repertory Theater (Indianapolis); "Young Abe Lincoln" (Lincoln Boyhood National Memorial); Marion Civic Theatre (Marion); Dunes Summer Theater (Michigan City); Canterbury Summer Theater (Michigan City); Brown County Playhouse (Nashville).

*The Circus City Festival in Peru displays circus costumes and paraphernalia. Peru served as winter quarters for several traveling circuses.*

## Famous People

Many famous people were born in the state of Indiana. Here are a few:

**Philip W. Anderson** b. 1923, Indianapolis. Nobel Prize-winning physicist

**Anne Baxter** 1923-1985, Michigan City. Academy Award-winning actress: *The Razor's Edge, All About Eve*

**Charles A. Beard** 1874-1948, near Knightstown. Historian

**Larry Bird** b. 1956, French Lick. Basketball player

**Bill Blass** b. 1922, Fort Wayne. Fashion designer

**Frank Borman** b. 1928, Gary. Astronaut

**Three Finger Brown** 1876-1948, Nyesville. Hall of Fame pitcher

**Ambrose Burnside** 1824-1881, Liberty. Union Army general

**Max Carey** 1890-1976, Terre Haute. Hall of Fame baseball player

**Hoagy Carmichael** 1899-1981, Bloomington. Song composer

**Oscar Charleston** 1896-1954, Indianapolis. Hall of Fame baseball player

**Eddie Condon** 1905-1973, Goodland. Jazz guitarist

**Adelle Davis** 1904-1974, Lizton. Nutritionist

**James Dean** 1931-1955, Marion. Film actor: *Rebel Without a Cause, Giant*

**Eugene Debs** 1855-1926, Terre Haute. Union leader

**Lloyd C. Douglas** 1877-1951, Columbia City. Novelist: *Magnificent Obsession, The Robe*

**Theodore Dreiser** 1871-1945, Terre Haute. Novelist: *Sister Carrie, An American Tragedy*

**Ray Ewry** 1873-1937, Lafayette. Track and field

*Ambrose Burnside, a Union Army general, eventually became governor of Rhode Island and served as a U.S. senator.*

athlete who won eight Olympic medals

**Ford Frick** 1894-1978, near Wawaka. Hall of Fame baseball executive

**Bernard F. Gimbel** 1885-1966, Vincennes. Department store executive

**Bob Griese** b. 1945, Evansville. Hall of Fame football quarterback

**Gus Grissom** 1926-1967, Mitchell. Astronaut

**Roy Halston** 1932-1990, Evansville. Fashion designer

**Richard G. Hatcher** b.1933, Michigan City. First black mayor of Gary

**Howard Hawks** 1896-1977, Goshen. Movie director: *To Have and Have Not, Rio Bravo*

**Jimmy Hoffa** 1913-1975, Brazil. Teamsters union president

**Michael Jackson** b. 1958, Gary. Pop singer

**J.J. Johnson** b. 1924, Indianapolis. Jazz trombonist

**Alex Karras** b. 1935, Gary. Football player, actor

**David Letterman** b. 1947, Indianapolis. Television talk show host

**Eli Lilly** 1885-1977, Indianapolis. Drug manufacturer and philanthropist

**Carole Lombard** 1908-1942, Fort Wayne. Film actress:

*Nothing Sacred, To Be or Not to Be*

**Wes Montgomery** 1925-1968, Indianapolis. Jazz guitarist

**Jane Pauley** b. 1950, Indianapolis. TV anchorwoman

**Cole Porter** 1893-1964, Peru. Composer of popular songs and musicals

**Ernie Pyle** 1900-1945, Dana. Pulitzer Prize-winning war correspondent

**James Whitcomb Riley** 1849-1916, Greenfield. Poet: *The Old Swimmin' Hole and 'Leven More Poems, Afterwhiles*

**Paul Samuelson** b. 1915, Gary. Nobel Prize-winning economist

**Rex Stout** 1886-1975, Noblesville. Mystery writer and creator of Nero Wolfe: *Black Orchids, The Doorbell Rang*

**Booth Tarkington** 1869-1946, Indianapolis. Two-time Pulitzer Prize-winning novelist: *The Magnificent Ambersons, Alice Adams*

**Twyla Tharp** b. 1941, Portland. Dancer and choreographer

**Kurt Thomas** b. 1956, Terre Haute. Olympic Gold Medal-winning gymnast

**Harold Urey** 1893-1981, Walkerton. Nobel Prize-winning chemist

**Kurt Vonnegut** b. 1922, Indianapolis. Novelist: *Slaughterhouse Five, Slapstick*

*Wilbur Wright and his brother Orville were pioneers of air travel. In 1903, they became the first to build and fly an engine-powered airplane.*

**Lew Wallace** 1827-1905, Brookville. Novelist: *Ben Hur*

**Jessamyn West** 1902-1984, near North Vernon. Novelist: *The Friendly Persuasion, A Matter of Time*

**Wendell Wilkie** 1892-1944, Elwood. Leader of the fight against isolationism during World War I

**Robert Wise** b. 1914, Winchester. Two-time Academy Award-winning movie director: *West Side Story, The Sound of Music*

**John Wooden** b. 1910, Martinsville. Named to the Basketball Hall of Fame both as a player and a coach

**Wilbur Wright** 1867-1912, near Millville. Co-designer of the first airplane

### Colleges and Universities

There are many colleges and universities in Indiana. Here are the most prominent, with their locations, dates of founding, and enrollments.

*Anderson College*, Anderson, 1917, 2,115

*Ball State University*, Muncie, 1918, 18,993

*Butler University*, Indianapolis, 1850, 4,187

*DePauw University*, Greencastle, 1837, 2,415

*Earlham College*, Richmond, 1847, 1,267

*Franklin College of Indiana*, Franklin, 1834, 801

*Goshen College*, Goshen, 1894, 1,152

*Hanover College*, Hanover, 827, 1,072

*Indiana Institute of Technology*, Fort Wayne, 1930, 902

*Fall foliage at Indiana University at Bloomington, one of many fine universities in the state.*

*Indiana State University*, Terre Haute, 1865, 12,005

*Indiana University, at Kokomo*, 1945, 3,438, South Bend, 1940, 6,981, Bloomington, 1820, 34,863, Richmond, 1971, 1570, Gary, 1959, 4,813, New Albany, 1941, 5,452.

*Indiana University-Purdue University at Fort Wayne*, 1917, 11,422, *at Indianapolis*, 1916, 26,649

*Indiana Wesleyan University*, Marion, 1920, 1,068

*Manchester College*, North Manchester, 1889, 1,100

*Marian College*, Indianapolis, 1851, 1,228

*Purdue University*, West Lafayette, 1869, 35,817, *Calumet*, Hammond 1951, 7,789, *North Central*, Westville, 1967, 3,351

*Rose-Hulman Institute of Technology*, Terre Haute, 1874, 1,420

*Saint Joseph's College*, Rensselaer, 1889, 1,001

*Saint Mary-of-the-Woods College*, Saint Mary-of-the-Woods, 1840, 910

*Saint Mary's College*, Notre Dame, 1844, 1,794

*Taylor University*, Upland, 1846, 1,708

*University of Notre Dame*, Notre Dame, 1842, 9,700

*University of Southern Indiana*, Evansville, 1965, 5,713

*Valparaiso University*, Valparaiso, 1859, 3,858

*Wabash College*, Crawfordsville, 1832, 832

**Where To Get More Information**

Indiana Department of Commerce
Tourism Development Division
One North Capitol Street
Suite 700
Indianapolis, IN 46204
Or call 1-800-289-6646

# Michigan

The Great Seal of Michigan was designed in 1835 and adopted in 1911. It is circular, and on it is a shield supported by an elk and a moose. On the shield is a man standing on a peninsula with his right hand raised and a rifle in his left. The sun is shining on him. On the top of the shield is the word *Tuebor*, which means "I will defend" in Latin. Under the seal is the state motto. Above the shield is an eagle holding an olive branch and three arrows. Around the seal is written "The Great Seal of the State of Michigan" and "A.D. MDCCCXXXV" — the date 1835 in Roman numerals — the year of the design of the seal and also the year that the first constitution of the state was framed.

### State Flag

The state flag of Michigan was adopted in 1911. It is blue, and in the center is the state seal.

### State Motto

*Si Quaeris Peninsulam Amoenam Circumspice*
The translation of this Latin motto is "If You Seek a Pleasant Peninsula, Look About You."

### State Pledge of Allegiance

Adopted in 1972, the state pledge of allegiance reads: "I pledge allegiance to the flag of Michigan, and to the state for which it stands, two beautiful peninsulas united by a bridge of steel, where equal opportunity and justice to all is our ideal."

*The lighhouse at Manistee, a Lake Michigan village that sits at the mouth of the Little Manistee River.*

### State Capital

Detroit was the capital of Michigan from 1835 to 1847, when the capital was moved to Ingham Township. A new capital city was built in what had been woods. First called Michigan, the town was shortly renamed Lansing. The first statehouse was a temporary one. A new brick building was built in 1854, with additions in 1863 and 1865. In 1871, the legislature set aside $1.2 million for a new capitol. This classical-revival style building was completed in 1879. The capitol is made of Ohio sandstone, Illinois limestone, Massachusetts granite, and Vermont marble. It has a magnificent dome and beautiful columns.

*The state capitol building in Lansing.*

Copper Harbor ■

*Keweenaw Bay*

N
△

ONTARIO

*LAKE SUPERIOR*

*Whitefish Bay*

SAULT SAINTE MARIE

OTTAWA NATIONAL FOREST

HIAWATHA NATIONAL FOREST

HIAWATHA NATIONAL FOREST

WISCONSIN

★ State Capital
● Cities or towns
■ OF SPECIAL INTEREST

■ MACKINAW CITY

*Green Bay*

■ Gaylord

*LAKE HURON*

Traverse City ■

HURON NATIONAL FOREST

**MICHIGAN**

MANISTEE NATIONAL FOREST

*Saginaw Bay*

Bay City ●

● Saginaw

*LAKE MICHIGAN*

Muskegon ●

**Grand Rapids** ●

● Wyoming

**Flint** ●

Port Huron ●

★ **Lansing**

Holland ●

Pontiac ●

*Lake Saint Clair*

■ Saugatuck

Battle Creek ●

**Detroit** ●

Kalamazoo ●

Jackson ●

■ DEARBORN

Ann Arbor ●

ILLINOIS

● Adrian

● Monroe

*LAKE ERIE*

INDIANA      OHIO

0    20      60      100 Miles
0   20   60   100   150 Kilometres

**State Name and Nicknames**

European explorers named Lake Michigan in 1672 after a clearing on the west side of the lower peninsula. In Ojibwa, the word for clearing is "majigan," and the state took the name of the lake.

Even though few Michiganders have ever seen the animal, the state is called the *Wolverine State* since wolverines used to roam the territory. Because of the Great Lakes that surround the state, it is also called the *Great Lakes State* and the *Lady of the Lake*. Finally, because of its prominence in the automotive industry, it is called the *Auto State*.

**State Flower**

The blossom of the apple tree, *Pyrus coronaria*, was named the state flower in 1897.

**State Tree**

*Pinus strobus*, the white pine, was adopted as the state tree in 1955. It is also

*The apple tree blossom is Michigan's state flower.*

called eastern white pine, northern white pine, soft pine, Weymouth pine, and spruce pine.

**State Bird**

In 1931, the robin, *Turdus migratorius*, was named the state bird.

**State Fish**

The trout, family *Salmonidae*, was adopted as the state fish in 1966.

**State Gem**

Named in 1973, the chlorastrolite, or greenstone, is the state gem.

**State Stone**

The Petoskey stone was adopted as state stone in 1966.

**State Song**

"Michigan, My Michigan," with words by Douglas Malloch and music by W. Otto Meissner, is the unofficial state song of Michigan.

**Population**

The population of Michigan in 1990 was 9,328,784, making it the eighth most populous state. There are 159.3 persons per square mile, 70.7 percent of

*The robin is the state bird.*

the population live in towns and cities. About 95 percent of the people in Michigan were born in the United States. Most of those born in other countries came from Canada. Other foreign-born groups include Poles, Italians, English, Germans, Russians, Scots, Dutch, Fins, and Swedes.

## Geography

Bounded on the north by Lake Superior, on the east by Lake Huron, the Canadian province of Ontario, and Lake Erie, on the south by Ohio and Indiana, and on the west by Lake Michigan and Wisconsin. Michigan has an area of 58,527 square miles, making it the 23rd largest state. The climate is hot in the summer and cold in the winter, because Michigan is surrounded by lakes which absorb heat from air warmer than themselves and warm colder winds.

The highest point in the state, at 1,980 feet, is atop

*A freighter sails past Isle Royale National Park in Lake Superior, the largest lake in the world.*

Mount Curwood in Baraga County, and the lowest, at 572 feet, is along the shore of Lake Erie. In the Lower Peninsula, low rolling plains give way to a rolling tableland of hilly belts. The Upper Peninsula is level in the east and rugged in the west. The major waterways of the state are the Escanaba, Manistique, Ontonagon, Sturgeon, Tahquamenon, Whitefish, Sable, Clinton,

Grand, Huron, Kalamazoo, Manistee, Muskegon, Raisin, Saginaw, St. Joseph, Detroit, St. Clair, St. Marys, Cass, and Pere Marquette rivers. Houghton Lake is the largest body of water inside the state.

## Industries

The principal industries of Michigan are mining, agriculture, food processing, and fishing. The chief

*Cars move along the assembly line in an auto plant in the Motor City, Detroit.*

### Government
The governor of Michigan serves a term of four years, as do the lieutenant governor, secretary of state, and attorney general. The state legislature consists of a 38-member senate and a 110-member house of representatives. Senators serve four-year terms, and representatives serve two-year terms. The most recent state constitution was adopted in 1964. In addition to its two U.S. senators, Michigan has 16 representatives in the U.S. House of Representatives. The state has 18 votes in the electoral college.

manufactured products are automobiles, machine tools, chemicals, cereals, metals and metal products, plastics, and furniture.

### Agriculture
The chief crops of the state are corn, winter wheat, soybeans, dry beans, oats, hay, sugar beets, honey, asparagus, potatoes, sweet corn, apples, cherries, grapes, peaches, and blueberries. Michigan is also a livestock state, and there are estimated to be some 1.4 million cattle, 1.2 million hogs and pigs, 108,000 sheep, and 8.9 million chickens and turkeys on its farms. Maple, oak, and aspen timber is cut. Iron ore, cement, crushed stone, sand, and gravel are important mineral resources. Commercial fishing brings in some $9.9 million a year.

### History
Before Europeans arrived, the land that was to become Michigan was populated by some 15,000 Indians. Most of them belonged to the Algonquin language group. They were the Ojibwa, Winnebago, and Menominee in the Upper Peninsula, and the Ottawa and Potawatomi in the Lower Peninsula. The

Wyandot, who lived near what is now Detroit, belonged to the Iroquois language group.

About 1620, the Frenchman Étienne Brulé explored the Upper Peninsula. In 1634, another Frenchman, Jean Nicolet, passed through on his way to find a route to the Pacific Ocean. In 1660, a mission was built at Keweenaw Bay by a French missionary, Father René Ménard. The first permanent settlements in Michigan were established at Sault Sainte Marie in 1668 by Father Jacques Marquette, and at Michilimackinac in 1671.

Other Frenchmen explored the region in the late 1600s. Among them were Louis Joliet and Robert Cavelier, Sieur de la Salle. By 1700, the French had established trading posts at several places on both peninsulas. In 1701, Fort Pontchartrain, which was to become Detroit, was founded by Antoine de la Mothe Cadillac. In 1763, after defeating the French in the French and Indian War, Great Britain gained control of Michigan; this was a time of bloody Indian wars in the region.

In 1774, Michigan became part of the Canadian province of Quebec. During the Revolutionary War, the British sent raiding parties from Detroit to attack American settlements. Spain was also fighting England at the time, and the Spanish captured Fort St. Joseph in Niles, but held it for only one day. Although the Revolution ended in 1783, the British did not surrender Detroit or Fort Mackinac until 1796, two years after they signed the John Jay Treaty.

In 1787, Michigan became part of the Northwest Territory of the United States. In 1800, part of Michigan

*Fort Michilimackinac, built in the earliest years of the eighteenth century, was an important fur-trading center as well as a battle site during the French and Indian Wars.*

joined with the Indiana Territory, and by 1803, all of Michigan was part of that territory. Congress established the Michigan Territory in 1805 with Detroit as the capital.

During the War of 1812, the British captured Detroit and Fort Mackinac, but they were returned to the United States when the war ended in 1814. In 1825, settlers began pouring in after the completion of the Erie Canal, which linked the eastern states with the western territories. In 1837, Michigan became the 26th state of the Union.

Iron ore mining began in the Upper Peninsula about 1845, and Michigan was on its way to becoming an industrial giant. During the Civil War, many Michiganders served with the Union forces. Indeed, it was the Fourth Michigan Cavalry that captured the president of the Confederacy, Jefferson Davis, in 1865.

After the war, lumbering became an important industry, as did the furniture business. Agriculture developed and railroads were built. In 1899, the Olds Motor Works opened in Detroit, and in 1903, Henry Ford opened his automobile factory.

During World War I, Michigan supplied the armed forces with trucks, armored vehicles, airplane engines, and other products. Michigan was hit hard by the Great Depression of the 1930s. Hundreds of thousands of workers lost their jobs. But during World War II, the auto industry was booming again—making airplanes, ships, tanks, and other military equipment. After the war, the automobile and copper-mining industries continued to prosper. Today, the state is an industrial giant that still manages to preserve vast areas of natural beauty.

*Fayette was a thriving iron-smelting village in the mid-nineteenth century. The town sits against a backdrop of white limestone cliffs.*

*The Palace of Auburn Hills is home to the Detroit Pistons of the National Basketball Association.*

## Sports

Historically, Michigan has always been a sports-minded state. The first professional hockey team was formed in Houghton in 1903. In 1959, Hamtramck won the Little League World Series. On the college level, the NCAA basketball championship has been won by both Michigan State University (1979) and the University of Michigan (1989). In football, the University of Michigan and Michigan State have both won Rose Bowl games. The NCAA baseball championship has been won by the University of Michigan in 1953 and 1962. The NCAA national championship in hockey has been won by the University of Michigan, Michigan State University, and Michigan Tech. On the professional level, the Detroit Tigers of the American League play baseball at Tiger Stadium. The Detroit Pistons of the National Basketball Association play in the Palace of Auburn Hills in Auburn Hills. The Detroit Lions of the National Football League appear at the Pontiac Silverdome in Pontiac. The Detroit Red Wings of the National Hockey League play in the Joe Louis Sports Arena.

## Major Cities

*Detroit* (population 1,203,339). Founded in 1701 by Antoine de la Mothe Cadillac at *le place du détroit*—"the place of the strait"—it soon became an important French trading post. It was captured by the British in 1760 and was not turned over to the United States until 1796. The British recaptured the town during the War of 1812. Detroit was finally incorporated in 1815. At the turn of the century the automobile boom transformed the city, as many immigrants came to Detroit to seek jobs.

*Things to see in Detroit:*
Mariners' Church (1848), Renaissance Center, People Mover, Washington Boulevard Trolley Car, Children's Museum, Detroit Institute of Arts, Detroit Historical Museum, Museum of African-American History, Detroit Public Library, Detroit Symphony Orchestra Hall, Detroit Science Center, Detroit Fire Department Historical Museum, Fisher Building, New Center One, Trinity Lutheran Church (1931), Historic Fort Wayne (1843-48), Detroit Zoo, Belle Isle, Whitcomb Conservatory, Safari-Trail Zoo, The Aquarium, Dossin Great Lakes Museum, Trappers Alley, Eastern Market (1892), and Boblo Island.

*Grand Rapids* (population 181,843). Settled in 1826 by Louis Campau as a trading post, the city gets its name from the rapids in the Grand River, which flows through the town. It is a city of furniture manufacturing, parks, and education.
*Things to see in Grand Rapids:*
Gerald R. Ford Museum, Grand Rapids Art Museum, Public Museum of Grand

*The Automobile in American Life is one exhibit at the Henry Ford Museum.*

Rapids, Grand Center, John Ball Zoo, Blandford Nature Center, *La Grande Vitesse*, a sculpture by Alexander Calder, and Fish Ladder.

*Lansing* (130,414). Settled in 1847, when the state capital moved here from Detroit, the city originally consisted of one log house and a sawmill. The city's industrial growth began when R. E. Olds

opened his Oldsmobile plant, and today it is a community of government and commerce.
*Things to see in Lansing:*
State Capitol, Michigan Historical Museum, Potter Park, Brenke River Sculpture and Fish Ladder, Carl G. Fenner Arboretum, Woldumar Nature Center, Impression 5 Science Museum, and R. E. Olds Transportation Museum.

**Places To Visit**
The National Park Service maintains seven areas in the state of Michigan: Isle Royale National Park, Sleeping Bear Dunes National Lakeshore, Pictured Rocks National Lakeshore, Hiawatha National Forest, Huron National Forest, Manistee National Forest, and Ottawa National Forest. In addition, there are 75 state recreation areas.
*Albion*: Gardner House Museum. Built in 1875, this is a restored Victorian home.
*Ann Arbor*: Kempf House. Built in 1853, this is an outstanding example of Greek Revival architecture.

**Battle Creek**: Leila Arboretum. This 72-acre park contains native trees and shrubs, as well as the Kingman Museum of Natural History.

**Bloomfield Hills**: Cranbrook Gardens. Forty acres of formal and informal gardens can be explored on winding trails.

**Cheboygan**: The U.S. Coast Guard Cutter *Mackinaw*. One of the world's largest icebreakers, the *Mackinaw* can be toured when she is in port.

**Copper Harbor**: Delaware Mine Tour. This copper mine dates back to the 1850s.

**Cranbrook Estate**: The estate of George G. Booth and Ellen Scripps Booth has become a cultural and educational center. It includes an art museum, gardens, a natural history museum, and several nationally known schools.

**Dearborn**: Henry Ford Museum and Greenfield Village. The museum and the buildings in the village contain thousands of historical artifacts, as well as the homes of the Wright Brothers and Henry Ford.

**Flint**: Crossroads Village/Huckleberry Railroad. This is a restored village of the 1860-80 period.

**Frankenmuth**: Michigan's Own, Military and Space Museum containing memorabilia of Michigan war heroes and astronauts.

**Gaylord**: Call of the Wild Museum. More than 150 life-size North American wild animals are displayed in scenic exhibits.

**Holland**: Dutch Village. Here are buildings of Dutch architecture, canals, windmills, street organs, and tulips.

**Iron Mountain**: Iron Mountain Iron Mine. Tours are conducted through the mine.

**Ishpeming**: National Ski Hall of Fame and Ski Museum. This houses national trophies and displays of old ski equipment.

**Kalamazoo**: Kalamazoo Air Zoo. Restored aircraft from World War II, many in flying condition, are on exhibit.

**Mackinac Island**: Fort Mackinac. The construction of this fort began in 1780. Mackinac Bridge is one of the world's longest suspension bridges.

**Mackinaw City**: Colonial Michilimackinac. The fortified colonial village of the mid-18th century has been reconstructed on original foundations.

**Muskegon**: USS *Silversides*. A World War II submarine with an impressive war record is open to the public.

**Port Austin**: Pioneer Huron City. Eight preserved buildings built in the 19th-century.

**Saginaw**: Saginaw Rose Garden. This is a spectacular circular garden with 1,000 rosebushes.

**Saugatuck**: SS *Keewatin*. The restored turn-of-the-century steamship is now a marine museum.

*The Mackinac Bridge joins Lake Michigan with Lake Huron.*

**Sault Ste. Marie**: Soo Locks Boat Tours. Here one can take a trip through both the American and Canadian locks, Lake Superior, and Lake Huron.

**Traverse City**: Schooner *Madeline*. This is a full-scale replica of an 1850 Great Lakes vessel.

*Putting on ice comes naturally to the people of Michigan, who host the Polar Ice Cap Golf Tournament every winter.*

## Events

There are many events and organizations that schedule activities of various kinds in the state of Michigan. Here are some of them:

*Sports:* MORC Sailboat Race (Alpena); Thimbleberry Blossom Festival (Copper Harbor); Grand Prix (Detroit); Polar Ice Cap Golf Tournament (Grand Haven); World's Championship Au Sable River Canoe Marathon (Grayling); Pine Mountain Ski Jumping Tournament (Iron Mountain); Upper Peninsula Championship Rodeo (Iron River); harness racing at Jackson Harness Raceway (Jackson); Michigan International Speedway (Jackson); White Pine Stampede (Mancelona); Pictured Rocks Road Race (Munising); Great Lakes International Sled Dog Race (Muskegon); Eagle Run Cross-Country Ski Race (Oscoda); Blue Water Festival/Mackinac Race (Port Huron); Tri-State Regatta (St. Joseph); Hobie Regatta (South Haven); Indian Summer Triathlon (Tawas City); Governor's Cup Hydroplane Races (Ypsilanti).

*Arts and Crafts:* Street Art Fair (Ann Arbor); Labor Day Arts Fair (Big Rapids); Waterfront Art Fair (Charlevoix); East Lansing Art Festival (East Lansing);

Kalamazoo County Flowerfest (Kalamazoo); Downtown Arts Festival (Lansing); Lilac Festival (Mackinac Island); Women's Club Antique Show (Mackinaw City); Art on the Rocks (Marquette); Arts Dockside (St. Ignace); Lake Bluff Art Fair (St. Joseph); Tawas Bay Waterfront Art Show (Tawas City).

*Music:* Ann Arbor Summer Festival (Ann Arbor); Cheboygan Opera House (Cheboygan); Tibbits Opera House (Coldwater); Michigan Opera Theatre (Detroit); Detroit Symphony (Detroit); Montreux Detroit Jazz Festival (Detroit); Flint Symphony (Flint); Music and Arts Festival (Grand Marais); Grand Rapids Symphony (Grand Rapids); National Music Camp (Interlochen); Kalamazoo Symphony (Kalamazoo); Lansing Symphony (Lansing); Hiawatha Music Co-op (Marquette); Matrix: Midland Festival (Midland); Great Lumbertown Music Festival (Muskegon); Meadow Brook Music Festival (Rochester); Saginaw Symphony (Saginaw); Frog Island Jazz Festival (Ypsilanti).

*Entertainment:* Highland Festival and Games (Alma); Alpena County Fair (Alpena); Cereal City Festival (Battle Creek); St. Stanislaus Polish

Festival (Bay City); Mayfest Festival (Bridgman); Apple Festival (Charlevoix); Northern Michigan Fair (Cheboygan); Winter Tip-Up Carnival (Coldwater); Muzzle Loaders Festival (Dearborn); Autumn Harvest Festival (Dearborn); International Auto Show (Detroit); International Freedom Festival (Detroit); Michigan State Fair (Detroit); Santa Claus Parade (Detroit); Riverfront Festivals (Detroit); Harbor Days (Elk Rapids); Upper Peninsula State Fair (Escanaba); Bavarian Festival (Frankenmuth); Winterfest (Gaylord); Alpenfest (Gaylord); Otsego County Fair (Gaylord); Venetian Boat Parade (Grand Haven); Milltown Festival (Grayling); Mushroom Festival (Harrison); Tulip Time Festival (Holland); Dickens Christmas (Holly); Winter Carnival (Houghton); Tip-Up-Town USA Ice Festival (Houghton Lake); Water Show (Iron Mountain); VJ Day (Iron River); Iron County Fair (Iron River); Rose Festival (Jackson); Civil War Muster and Battle Re-enactment (Jackson); Jackson County Fair (Jackson); Maple Sugaring Weekend (Kalamazoo); Michigan International Air Show (Kalamazoo); Wine and Harvest Festival (Kalamazoo); Festival of the Pines (Lake City); Riverfest (Lansing); Colonial

Michilimackinac Pageant (Mackinaw City); Voyageur's Rendezvous (Mackinaw City); Polish Heritage Festival (Manistee); International Food Festival (Marquette); Waterfront Festival (Menominee); Monroe County Fair (Monroe); Old French Town Days (Monroe); Four Flags Area Apple Festival (Niles); Onekama Days (Onekama); Indian Powwow (Petoskey); Emmet County Fair (Petoskey); Island City Festival (Plainwell); Ice Sculpture Spectacular (Plymouth); Feast of the Ste. Claire (Port Huron); Mitas Polka Fest (Saginaw); Antique Car Show (St. Ignace); Mint Festival (St. Johns); Blossomtime Festival (St. Joseph); Harbor Days (Saugatuck); National Blueberry Festival (South Haven); MarinerFest (Tawas City); Cherry Festival (Traverse City).

*Tours*: Historic Home Tour (Marshall); Wurtsmith Air Force Base Tours (Oscoda); Historic Home Tours (Owosso).

*Theater*: Calumet Theater (Calumet); Tibbits Professional Summer Theatre Series (Coldwater); The Theater Company-University of Detroit (Detroit); Community Circle Theater (Grand Rapids); Kalamazoo Civic Players (Kalamazoo); Ramsdell Theater (Manistee); Midland Center for

*The Fox Theater is a beautifully renovated auditorium in Detroit where touring productions are performed.*

the Arts (Midland); Meadow Brook Theatre (Rochester); Cherry County Playhouse (Traverse City).

## Famous People

Many famous people were born in the state of Michigan. Here are a few:

**Nelson Algren** 1909-1981, Detroit. Novelist: *The Man*

*Thomas E. Dewey practiced law before he was elected governor of New York; he lost presidential campaigns to Franklin D. Roosevelt and Harry Truman.*

with the Golden Arm, A Walk on the Wild Side

**George Allen** 1922-1990, Detroit. Football coach

**Sonny Bono** b. 1935, Detroit. Pop singer

**Avery Brundage** 1887-1975, Detroit. President of the International Olympic Committee

**Ralph Bunche** 1904-1971, Detroit. Nobel Prize-

winning diplomat

**Bruce Catton** 1899-1978, Petoskey. Historian

**Alice Cooper** b. 1948, Detroit. Rock singer

**Francis Ford Coppola** b. 1939, Detroit. Academy Award-winning producer-director-writer: *The Godfather, Apocalypse Now*

**Dave DeBusschere** b. 1940, Detroit. Hall of Fame basketball player

**Thomas E. Dewey** 1902-1971, Owosso. Governor and presidential candidate

**John F. Dodge** 1864-1920, Niles. Automobile manufacturer

**Edna Ferber** 1887-1968, Kalamazoo. Pulitzer Prize-winning novelist: *So Big, Giant*

**Edsel Ford** 1893-1943, Detroit. Automobile manufacturer

**Henry Ford** 1863-1947, Wayne County. Automobile manufacturer

**Henry Ford II** 1917-1987, Detroit. Automobile

manufacturer

**Harvey Fruehauf** 1893-1968, Grosse Pointe Park. Truck trailer manufacturer

**Frank Gerber** 1873-1952, Douglas. Baby food manufacturer

**Julie Harris** b. 1925, Grosse Pointe. Five-time Tony Award-winning actress: *The Member of the Wedding*

*Will Keith Kellogg was a cereal manufacturer who promoted cornflakes as a healthy and convenient breakfast food in the early 1900s.*

**James Leo Herlihy** b. 1927, Detroit. Novelist: *All Fall Down, Midnight Cowboy*

**Alfred D. Hershey** b. 1908, Owosso. Nobel Prize-winning biologist

**John Harvey Kellogg** 1852-1945, Tyrone. Founded idea of mass produced healthy food in the U.S.

**Will Keith Kellogg** 1860-1951, Battle Creek. Cereal manufacturer

**Ring Lardner** 1885-1933, Niles. Short-story writer: *You Know Me, Al; Gullible's Travels*

**Charles A. Lindbergh** 1902-1974, Detroit. First man to fly solo across the Atlantic

**Ed McMahon** b. 1923, Detroit. TV announcer and host

**Michael Moriarty** b. 1941, Detroit. Emmy Award-winning actor: *Holocaust, The Hanoi Hilton*

**Joy Morton** 1855-1934, Detroit. Salt manufacturer

**Della Reese** b. 1931, Detroit. Jazz singer

*Charles A. Lindbergh piloted the first nonstop flight from New York to Paris on* The Spirit of St. Louis *in 1927.*

**Sugar Ray Robinson** 1921-1989, Detroit. Welterweight and middleweight boxing champion

**Theodore Roethke** 1908-1963, Saginaw. Pulitzer Prize-winning poet: *The Waking, Words for the Wind*

**Diana Ross** b. 1944, Detroit. Pop singer

**Glenn Seaborg** b. 1912, Ishpeming. Nobel Prize-winning chemist

**Potter Stewart** b. 1915, Jackson. U.S. Supreme Court justice

**Danny Thomas** 1914-1991, Deerfield. Comedian

**Marlo Thomas** b. 1943, Detroit. Television and stage actress: *That Girl, Thieves*

**Lily Tomlin** b. 1939, Detroit. Film actress and comedian: *Nashville, 9 to 5*

**Thomas H. Weller** b. 1915, Ann Arbor. Nobel Prize-winning microbiologist

**Stevie Wonder** b. 1950, Saginaw. Rock-blues singer

**Sheila Young** b. 1950, Birmingham. Olympic speed skater

**Colleges and Universities**

There are many colleges and universities in Michigan. Here are the more prominent, with their locations, dates of founding, and enrollments.

*Adrian College,* Adrian, 1845, 1,207

*Albion College*, Albion, 1835, 1,700

*Alma College*, Alma, 1886, 1,241

*Aquinas College*, Grand Rapids, 1886, 2,625

*Calvin College*, Grand Rapids, 1876, 4,325

*Central Michigan University*, Mount Pleasant, 1892, 17,229

*Detroit College of Business Administration*, Dearborn, 1936, 2,625

*Eastern Michigan University*, Ypsilanti, 1849, 24,807

*Ferris State College*, Big Rapids, 1884, 11,847

*Hillsdale College*, Hillsdale, 1844, 1,102

*Hope College*, Holland, 1851, 2,770

*Kalamazoo College*, Kalamazoo, 1833, 1,255

*Madonna College*, Livonia, 1937, 4,064

*Marygrove College*, Detroit, 1906, 1,230

*Mercy College of Detroit*, Detroit, 1941, 2,218

*Michigan State University*, East Lansing, 1855, 42,866

*Michigan Technological University*, Houghton, 1885, 6,662

*Northern Michigan University*, Marquette, 1899, 8,375

*Oakland University*, Rochester, 1959, 12,385

*Olivet College*, Olivet, 1844, 766

*Siena Heights College*, Adrian, 1919, 1,572

*University of Detroit*, Detroit, 1877, 5,832

*University of Michigan*, Ann Arbor, 1817, 36,338; Dearborn, 1959, 6,707; Flint, 1956, 6,506

*Wayne State University*, Detroit, 1868, 32,477

*Western Michigan University*, Kalamazoo, 1903, 26,315

**Where To Get More Information**
The Travel Bureau
Michigan Department of Commerce
Box 30226
Lansing, MI 48909
Or call 1-800-5432-YES

# Ohio

The Seal of Ohio was adopted in 1868 and revised in 1967. It is circular and features a bundle of 17 arrows on the left (symbolizing Ohio's admission to the Union as the 17th state) and a sheaf of wheat on the right (standing for the richness of Ohio's land). Above them is the sun rising behind Mount Logan, commemorating Ohio's distinction as the first state west of the Allegheny Mountains. On the outer rim of the seal is "The Great Seal of the State of Ohio."

**State Flag**

The state flag of Ohio is pennant-shaped. On a background of five stripes (three red and two white) is a triangle. In the triangle is a white circle (standing for O, the state's initial) with a red center (standing for the buckeye nut). Also on the triangle are 17 stars, since Ohio was the 17th state.

**State Motto**

*With God, All Things Are Possible*

This motto, which was adopted in 1959, comes from the Bible (Matthew 19:26).

*Germantown preserves many of the structures of Columbus's largest nineteenth-century ethnic group.*

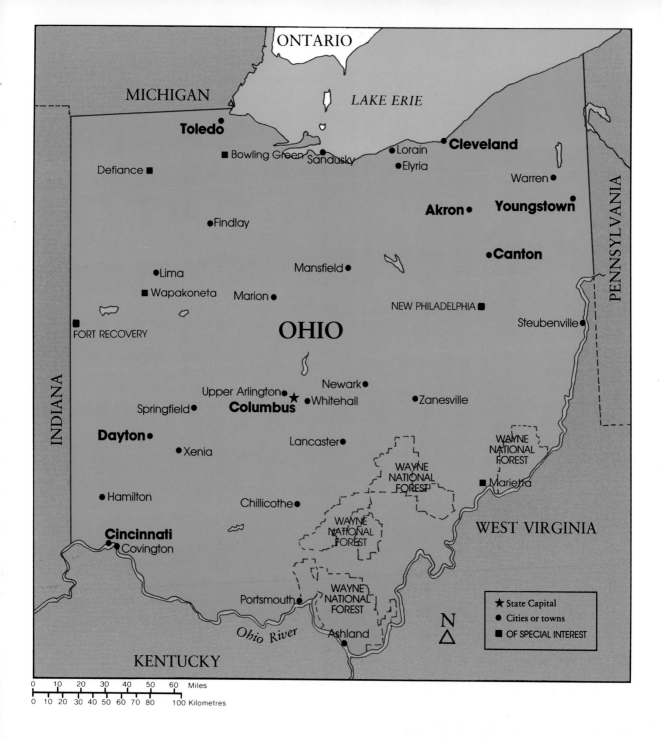

*The state capitol building in Columbus.*

## State Capital

The first capital of Ohio was Chillicothe (1803-10). Then came Zanesville (1810-12), and Chillicothe again (1812-16). In 1817, the state legislature voted to relocate the capital in Columbus, which had no name at the time. The first statehouse in Columbus was destroyed by fire in 1852. The present capitol building was completed in 1861 for $1,359,121, and an annex was added in 1901. This Greek Revival building has Doric columns and is built of limestone.

### State Name and Nicknames

In 1680, the French explorer Robert Cavelier, Sieur de la Salle, noted that the Iroquois Indians called the large river on the southern boundary of the area "Ohio," which meant "large [or] beautiful river." The state was then named after the river.

The most common nickname for Ohio is the *Buckeye State*, partly because of the many buckeye trees in the state and partly because of an incident that occurred in 1788. One of the colonial commanders, Colonel Sproat, was so tall that the Indians called him "Big Buckeye." Ohio is also referred to as the *Mother of Modern Presidents*, because seven U.S. presidents were born in the state.

### State Flower

The scarlet carnation (family *Caryophyllaceae*) was adopted as Ohio's state flower in 1904 in memory of former President William McKinley, who thought of the flower as a good luck charm.

### State Tree

In 1953, the buckeye tree, *Aesculus glabra*, was named state tree. The buckeye got its name from Indians, who thought the seed of the tree looked like the eye of the buck, or "hetuck." Other names for the tree are Ohio buckeye, fetid buckeye, stinking buckeye, and American horse chestnut.

### State Bird

The cardinal, *Cardinalis cardinalis*, was designated the state bird in 1933.

*The scarlet carnation was adopted in 1904 as Ohio's state flower.*

*The cardinal is the state bird.*

### State Animal

The white-tailed deer, *Odocoileus virginianus*, was adopted as the state animal in 1988.

### State Insect

The Ladybird Beetle or common ladybug, was named state insect in 1975.

### State Beverage

Tomato juice was named state beverage in 1965.

### State Gem

Ohio flint was adopted as state gem in 1965.

### State Song

"Beautiful Ohio" was

adopted as the state song in 1969. It was written in 1918 by Ballard MacDonald, with music by Robert S. King. In 1989, the Ohio legislature adopted an amendment of the Ohio Revised Code that changed the words of the state song. The new lyrics are by Wilbert McBride.

## Population

The population of Ohio in 1990 was 10,887,325, making it the seventh most populous state. There are 263.4 persons per square mile, 73.3 percent of the population live in towns and cities. More than 97 percent of Ohioans were born in the United States. Most of those born in other countries came from Czechoslovakia, England, Germany, Hungary, Italy, and Poland.

## Geography

Bounded on the north by Michigan and Lake Erie, on the east by Pennsylvania and West Virginia, on the south by Kentucky, and on the west by Indiana, Ohio has an area of 41,330 square miles, making it the 35th largest state. The climate is temperate and variable.

Most of the state is gentle rolling plains. The Allegheny Plateau can be found in the east and the central plain in the west. The highest point in the state is Campbell Hill, 1,550 feet, in Logan County. The lowest point, at 433 feet, is in Hamilton County in the southeast. The major waterways in Ohio are the Maumee, Ohio, Miami, Hocking, Little Miami, Mahoning, Muskingum, Scioto, Cuyahoga, Grand, Huron, Portage, Sandusky, and Vermilion rivers. The largest lake in Ohio is Grand Lake.

## Industries

The principal industries of the state of Ohio are manufacturing and trade.

*Sailboats navigate the placid waters of Lake Erie, which forms part of the northern border of Ohio.*

The chief manufactured products are transportation equipment, machinery, and metal products. Other products are iron, steel, rubber, automobiles, heavy machinery, electrical and electronic components and appliances, chemicals, plastic, glass, pottery and clay products.

## Agriculture

The chief crops of the state are corn, hay, winter wheat, oats, and soybeans. Ohio is also a livestock state; there are estimated to be some 1.8 million cattle, 2 million hogs and pigs, 275,000 sheep, and 22 million chickens and turkeys on its farms. Oak, ash, maple, walnut, and beech trees are cut. Crushed stone, sand, gravel, lime, clays, and cement are important mineral resources. Commercial fishing brings in some $1.3 million per year.

*Robotics is just one of the many industries that contributes to Ohio's economy.*

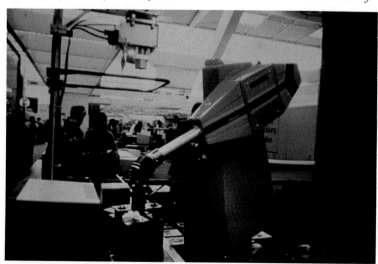

## Government

The governor of Ohio is elected to a four-year term. The state legislature, or general assembly, which meets in odd-numbered years, consists of a senate and a house of representatives. Senators are elected to four-year terms, and representatives to two-year terms. The total number of senators and representatives is not spelled out in the state constitution. In addition to its two U.S. senators, Ohio has 19 representatives in the U.S. House of Representatives. The state has 21 votes in the electoral college. The most recent state constitution was adopted in 1851.

## History

Before Europeans arrived, what was to become Ohio was inhabited by prehistoric Indians called Adena, Hopewell, and Mississippian peoples. Later, they were replaced by Erie, Miami, Shawnee, and Wyandot Indians.

*Oliver Hazard Perry defeated the British at the Battle of Lake Erie on September 10, 1813.*

Robert Cavelier, Sieur de la Salle, a French explorer, may have been the first European to visit present-day Ohio, in 1670. Following his explorations, France claimed all of the Northwest. But the British also claimed all the territory west of their eastern colonies. In 1750, Christopher Gist was sent by the Ohio Company of Virginia to explore the upper Ohio River Valley. After the French and Indian War, France gave

*Alfred E. Mathews sketched this drawing on the spot at The Battle of Wild Cat during the Civil War, in October, 1861.*

Great Britain sovereignty over most of its land east of the Mississippi River.

During the Revolutionary War, fighting forced a Moravian settlement, Schoenbrunn (near today's New Philadelphia), to be abandoned in 1776. In 1780, George Rogers Clark defeated pro-British Indians in the Battle of Piqua (near today's Springfield).

The region including Ohio became part of the Northwest Territory in 1787. In 1788, Marietta, the first permanent settlement in Ohio, was founded, and the town became the first capital of the Northwest Territory. Indian uprisings followed, and General Anthony Wayne put down the insurrection in the Battle of Fallen Timbers (near today's Toledo) in 1794. Ohio became the 17th state of the Union in 1803.

During the War of 1812, Commodore Oliver H. Perry

defeated the British fleet in Lake Erie off the Ohio shore. New settlers and new industry and agriculture were encouraged by the completion of the Erie Canal in 1825 and the Ohio and Erie Canal (Cleveland to Portsmouth) in 1832. Then came the Miami and Erie Canal (Toledo to Cincinnati) in 1845. After that, railroads were also built.

During the Civil War, Ohio supplied about 345,000 men to the Union army. After the war, industry boomed in the state, as did agriculture and transportation. During World War I, Ohio supplied vast amounts of war materials, and some 256,000 Ohioans served in the armed forces.

Farmers lost their farms and workers lost their jobs during the Great Depression of the 1930s. Then came World War II, and some 839,000 Ohio men and women served in the armed forces. There were training centers in the state, and huge amounts of steel, tires, and other war materials were produced.

Today, Ohio's industrial growth is expanding, but it is still a state of great beauty.

## Sports

Ohio has always been a hotbed of sports. The first professional baseball team—the Cincinnati Red Stockings—was formed in 1869. On the collegiate level, Ohio State and the University of Cincinnati have won NCAA national basketball championships. In collegiate football, Ohio State, a perennial football power, has made many post-season bowl appearances. On the professional level, the Cincinnati Reds of the National League play baseball in Riverfront Stadium, and the Cincinnati Bengals of the National Football League share the facility. The Cleveland Indians of the American League play baseball in Cleveland Stadium. They share the facility with the Cleveland Browns of the National Football League. The Cleveland Cavaliers of the National Basketball Association play in the Coliseum in nearby Richfield.

## Major Cities

*Cincinnati* (population 385,457). Settled in 1788, it was originally called Losantiville. During the early 1800s, many immigrants

*Ohio State football is a popular pastime for the state's sports fans.*

moved in, most of them Germans. Cincinnati was soon to become a bustling frontier riverboat town. Today it is a city with charm, culture, and fine food.

*Things to see in Cincinnati:* Cincinnati Zoo and Botanical Garden, Carew Tower, Hamilton County Courthouse, Public Landing, City Hall (1888), William Howard Taft National

Historic Site, Harriet Beecher Stowe Memorial, John Hauck House Museum, Loveland Castle, Contemporary Arts Center, Cincinnati Fire Museum, Taft Museum (1820), Mount Airy Forest and

*A view of the brilliantly-lit skyline of Cincinnati, the state's third-largest metropolitan area.*

Arboretum, Civic Garden Center of Greater Cincinnati, Mount Adams, Museum of Natural History and Planetarium, Cincinnati Art Museum, and Sharon Woods Village.

*Cleveland* (population 573,822). Founded in 1796 by Moses Cleveland, the town soon began to profit from Great Lakes transportation, and later became a bustling industrial town. Today, Ohio's most populous city still retains the charm of wide streets, 39 city parks and 17,500 acres of metropolitan parks.

*Things to see in Cleveland:*
City Hall, Federal Buildings, Public Square, USS *Cod,* Dunham Tavern Museum, Cleveland Health Education Museum, Lake View Cemetery, Cleveland Museum of Art, Cleveland Museum of Natural History, Ralph Mueller Planetarium, the Western Reserve Historical Society Museum and Library, Frederick C. Crawford Auto-Aviation Museum, Wade Park and Garden Center, Cultural Gardens, Rockefeller

Greenhouse, Temple Museum of Religious Art, Dittrick Museum of Medical History, Cleveland Metroparks Zoo, and NASA Lewis Visitor Center.

*Columbus* (population 565,032). Founded in 1812, Columbus was created and laid out to be the capital of Ohio. By 1833, the new National Road reached the town and it began to grow. Today, it is a most attractive city, with broad tree-lined streets and beautiful parks.

*Things to see in Columbus:*
Ohio State Capitol, McKinley Memorial, City Hall, Camp Chase Confederate Cemetery, Ohio Historical Center, Ohio Village, Ohio's Center of Science and Industry, Columbus Museum of Art, Ohio Railway Museum, German Village, Columbus Zoological Gardens, Park of Roses, Chadwick Arboretum, and Franklin Park Conservatory and Garden Center.

**Places to Visit**

The National Park Service maintains four areas in the

state of Ohio: Mound City Group National Monument, Perry's Victory and International Peace Memorial, William Howard Taft Birthplace, and Wayne National Forest. In addition, there are 65 state recreation areas.

*Akron*: Stan Hywet Hall and Gardens. This Tudor revival

*Cleveland's location on Lake Erie helped make it a major industrial city.*

*Canton is home to the Professional Football Hall of Fame, where visitors can learn the history of the game and see its great collection of memorabilia.*

mansion, with 65 rooms, contains antiques and art treasures.

*Ashtabula*: Great Lakes Marine and U.S. Coast Guard Memorial Museum. Many maritime exhibits are displayed in the 1898 lighthouse keeper's home.

*Aurora*: Sea World. This marine-life park has regular shows, with killer whales, dolphins, seals, and sea otters.

*Bowling Green*: Educational Memorabilia Center. More than 1,500 historic educational items are displayed in a restored one-room schoolhouse.

*Canton*: Pro Football Hall of Fame. Thousands of items of professional football memorabilia are on display here.

*Coshocton*: Roscoe Village Restoration. This restoration of a busy town on the Ohio-Erie Canal, settled in 1816, includes the Toll House with model locks.

*Dayton*: Wright Cycle Shop. This is a replica of the shop where the Wright Brothers performed their experiments

in aviation. United States Air Force Museum.

*Defiance*: Au Glaize Village. Replicas and restored 19th-century buildings include a railroad station with rolling stock.

*Delaware*: Olentangy Indian Caverns and Ohio Frontierland. This is a natural limestone cave and Indian village.

*Mansfield*: Kingwood Center and Gardens. Here are 49 acres of landscaped gardens and greenhouses.

*Marietta*: Campus Martius and Museum of the Northwest Territory. Historic buildings from the 1700s.

*Marion*: President Warren G. Harding's Home and Museum.

*Mason*: Kings Island. This 1600-acre family entertainment center contains a zoo and more than 40 rides.

*New Philadelphia*: Zoar State Memorial. The quaint village, where German religious separatists sought refuge in 1817, was an experiment in communal living for 80 years.

*Sandusky*: Cedar Point. An amusement park with 54 rides and live shows near a mile-long beach and marina.

*Springfield*: Westcott House. This 1908 home was designed by Frank Lloyd Wright.

*Strongsville*: Gardenview Horticultural Park. Here are 16 acres of English-style gardens with rare plants.

*Toledo*: Toledo Zoological Gardens. More than 2,000 animals are on display here.

*Wapakoneta*: Neil Armstrong Air and Space Museum. Aircraft including balloons and the Gemini 8 capsule in which Armstrong accomplished the first spacecraft docking in orbit are displayed here.

*Warren*: John Stark Edwards House. Built in 1807, this is the oldest house in the Western Reserve.

*Wauseon*: Sauder Farm and Craft Village. Farmstead and pioneer village with craft demonstrations.

## Events

There are many events and organizations that schedule activities of various kinds in the state of Ohio. Here are some of them.

*Sports*: All-American Soapbox Derby (Akron); NEC "World Series of Golf" (Akron); National Jigsaw Puzzle Championship (Athens); National Tractor Pulling Championship (Bowling Green); International Chicken Flying Meet (Gallipolis); Four Wheeler Rodeo (Lisbon); Ohio Ski Carnival (Mansfield); auto racing at Mid-Ohio Sports Car Course (Mansfield); National Archery Tournament (Oxford); National Matches (Port Clinton); Charity Horse Show (Portsmouth); Grand American Tournament of the Amateur Trapshooting Association of America (Vandalia).

*Arts and Crafts*: Carnation Festival (Alliance); Ohio Hills Folk Festival (Cambridge); Salt Forks Arts and Crafts Festival (Cambridge); Tri-State Pottery Festival (East Liverpool); Zane Square Arts and Crafts Festival (Lancaster); Square Fair/Summer Community Arts Festival (Lima); Indian Summer Arts and Crafts Festival (Marietta).

*Music*: Ohio Ballet (Akron); Akron Symphony (Akron); Blossom Music Center (Akron); Canton Symphony (Canton); Canton Ballet (Canton); Canton Civic Opera (Canton); Cincinnati Ballet Company (Cincinnati); Cincinnati Opera Association (Cincinnati); Cincinnati Symphony (Cincinnati); May Festival (Cincinnati); Riverfront Stadium Festival (Cincinnati);

*The rollercoaster loops of Cedar Point are only one attraction at the amusement park in Sandusky.*

Cleveland Ballet (Cleveland); Cleveland Opera (Cleveland); Cleveland Orchestra (Cleveland); Ballet Met (Columbus); Stuart Pimsler Dance and Theater (Columbus); Opera/Columbus (Columbus); Columbus Symphony (Columbus); Greater Columbus Arts Festival (Columbus); Dulcimer Days (Coshocton); Dayton Philharmonic (Dayton); Concerts at the Dayton Art Institute (Dayton); Summer Series of Concerts (Dayton); Zivili Kolo Ensemble (Granville); US Open Drum and Bugle Corps Competition (Marion); Jamboree in the Hills (St. Clairsville); Toledo Symphony (Toledo); Youngstown Symphony (Youngstown).

*Entertainment*: Train Meet (Akron); Wonderful World of Ohio Mart (Akron); Harvest Festival (Akron); Cherry Festival (Bellevue); Bratwurst Festival (Bucyrus); Celina Lake Festival (Celina); Geauga County Maple Festival (Chardon); Fall Festival of Leaves (Chillicothe); Riverfest (Cincinnati); International Folk Festival (Cincinnati); Ohio State Fair (Columbus); Columbus Day Celebration (Columbus); Coshocton Canal Festival (Coshocton); River Festival (Dayton); Dayton Air and Trade Show (Dayton); Flowing Rivers Festival (Defiance); Geneva Grape Jamboree (Geneva-on-the-Lake); Fort Hamilton Days Festival (Hamilton); Antique Car Parade (Hamilton); Tri-State Fair and Regatta (Ironton); Spring Old Car Festival (Lancaster); Lancaster Festival (Lancaster); Ohio Honey Festival (Lebanon); Johnny Appleseed Festival (Lisbon); International Festival Week (Lorain); Ohio River Sternwheel Festival (Marietta); Popcorn Festival (Marion); Zoar Harvest Festival (New Philadelphia); Swiss Festival (New Philadelphia); Heritage Festival (Piqua); Roy Rogers Convention and Western Festival (Portsmouth); Portsmouth Sternwheel Regatta and Festival (Portsmouth); River Days Festival (Portsmouth); International Festival (Toledo); Northwest Ohio Rib-Off (Toledo); Fall Folk Festival (Toledo); Zane's Trace Commemoration (Zanesville).

*Tours*: Pilgrimage Tour of 19th-Century homes (Lancaster); Christmas Candlelight Tours (Lancaster); Hocking Hills Fall Color Caravan Tour (Logan).

*Theater*: Ohio Valley Summer Theater (Athens); The Living Word Outdoor Drama (Cambridge); "Tecumseh!"

*The Pumpkin Festival in Circleville is a fall tradition.*

*Tecumseh! is an outdoor drama production in Chillicothe, a town that takes its name from Chahlagawtha, a Shawnee village that occupied that site.*

(Chillicothe); Cincinnati Playhouse in the Park (Cincinnati); Cleveland Play House (Cleveland); Actors Summer Theater (Columbus); Lakewood Little Theater (Lakewood); Showboat Becky Thatcher (Marietta); "Trumpet in the Land" (New Philadelphia); Youngstown Playhouse (Youngstown).

### Famous People

Many famous people were born in the state of Ohio. Here are a few:

**Sherwood Anderson** 1876-1941, Camden. Novelist: *Winesburg, Ohio; Dark Laughter*

**Eddie Arcaro** b. 1916, Cincinnati. Jockey

**Neil Armstrong** b. 1930, Wapakoneta. Astronaut

**Erma Bombeck** b. 1927, Dayton. Columnist

**Paul Brown** b. 1908, Norwalk. Hall of Fame football coach

**Arthur H. Compton** 1892-1962, Wooster. Nobel Prize-winning physicist

**Powel Crosley, Jr.** 1886-1961, Cincinnati. Industrialist and owner of the Cincinnati Reds

**Hart Crane** 1899-1932, Garrettsville. Poet: *The Bridge, White Buildings*

**George A. Custer** 1839-1876, New Rumley. Union Army officer and Indian fighter

**Clarence Darrow** 1857-1938, near Kinsman. Lawyer

**Charles G. Dawes** 1865-1951, Marietta. Nobel Prize-winning diplomat

**Len Dawson** b. 1935, Alliance. Hall of Fame football player

**Doris Day** b. 1924, Cincinnati. Movie actress: *The Pajama Game, That Touch of Mink*

**Phyllis Diller** b. 1917, Lima. Comedienne

**Hugh Downs** b. 1921, Akron. TV newsman

**Thomas Edison** 1847-1931,

*Thomas Edison, who invented the light bulb and the phonograph, was granted over 1,000 patents during his life.*

Milan. Inventor of the light bulb

**Suzanne Farrell** b. 1945, Cincinnati. Ballerina

**Harvey Firestone** 1868-1938, Columbiana. Tire manufacturer

**Clark Gable** 1901-1960, Cadiz. Academy Award-winning actor: *It Happened One Night, Gone with the Wind*

**James N. Gamble** 1836-1932, Cincinnati. Soap manufacturer

**James A. Garfield** 1831-1881, near Orange. Twentieth President of the United States

**John Glenn** b. 1921, Cambridge. Astronaut and U.S. senator

**David M. Goodrich** 1876-1950, Akron. Tire manufacturer

**Ulysses S. Grant** 1822-1885, Point Pleasant. Eighteenth President of the United States

**Joel Grey** b. 1932, Cleveland. Academy Award-winning actor: *Cabaret, Remo Williams: The Adventure Begins*

**Warren G. Harding** 1865-1923, Blooming Grove. Twenty-ninth President of the United States

**Benjamin Harrison** 1833-1901, North Bend. Twenty-third President of the United States

**John Havlicek** b. 1940,

Martins Ferry. Hall of Fame basketball player

**Rutherford B. Hayes** 1822-1893, Delaware. Nineteenth President of the United States

**Zane Grey** 1875-1939, Zanesville. Western novelist: *The Last of the Plainsmen, Riders of the Purple Sage*

**Kenesaw Mountain Landis** 1866-1944, Millville. Commissioner of baseball

*Suzanne Farrell was a star of the New York City Ballet.*

**James Levine** b. 1943, Cincinnati. Opera conductor

**James Lovell** b. 1928, Cleveland. Astronaut

**Henry Mancini** b. 1924, Cleveland. Song composer

**William H. Masters** b. 1915, Cleveland. Sexologist

**William McKinley** 1843-1901, Niles. Twenty-fifth President of the United States

**Edwin Moses** b. 1953, Dayton. Olympic gold medal-winning hurdler

**Paul Newman** b. 1925, Cleveland. Academy Award-winning actor: *The Color of Money, The Verdict*

**Jack Nicklaus** b. 1940, Columbus. Championship golfer

**Ransom E. Olds** 1864-1950, Geneva. Auto manufacturer

**James W. Packard** 1863-1928, Warren. Auto manufacturer

**Norman Vincent Peale** b. 1898, Bowersville. Clergyman

*Rutherford B. Hayes served in the Civil War and was governor of Ohio for two terms before he was elected president in 1877.*

**Tyrone Power** 1914-1958, Cincinnati. Film actor: *The Sun Also Rises, Witness for the Prosecution*

**Sally Priesand** b. 1946, Cleveland. First American woman rabbi

**William Proctor** 1862-1934, Glendale. Soap manufacturer

**Charles F. Richter** 1900-1985, near Hamilton. Seismologist and developer of the Richter Scale

**Eddie Rickenbacker** 1890-1973, Columbus. World War I air ace

**Branch Rickey** 1881-1965, Stockdale. Hall of Fame baseball executive

**John D. Rockefeller, Jr.** 1874-1960, Cleveland. Philanthropist

**Roy Rogers** b. 1912, Cincinnati. Film cowboy star

**Pete Rose** b. 1941, Cincinnati. Baseball player and manager

**Arthur Schlesinger** b. 1917, Columbus. Historian

**Martin Sheen** b. 1940, Dayton. Film actor: *Apocalypse Now, The Dead Zone*

**William Tecumseh Sherman** 1820-1891, Lancaster. Union general

**Roger Staubach** b. 1942, Cincinnati. Hall of Fame football quarterback

**Gloria Steinem** b. 1934, Toledo. Feminist writer

**William Howard Taft** 1857-1930, Cincinnati. Twenty-seventh President of the United States and chief justice of the Supreme Court

**Art Tatum** 1910-1956, Toledo. Jazz pianist

**Tecumseh** 1768-1813, Greene County. Shawnee Indian chief

**Norman Thomas** 1884-1968, Marion. Co-founder of the American Civil Liberties Union

**James Thurber** 1894-1961, Columbus. Humorist: *My Life and Hard Times, The Years with Ross*

**Ted Turner** b. 1938, Cincinnati. Communications executive

**Paul Warfield** b. 1942, Warren. Hall of Fame football player

**Jonathan Winters** b. 1925, Dayton. Television and film comedian: *The Loved One, Viva Max*

**Victoria Woodhull** 1838-1927, Homer. First woman candidate for president

**Orville Wright** 1871-1948, Dayton. Co-developer of the airplane

**Cy Young** 1867-1955, Gilmore. Hall of Fame baseball pitcher

## Colleges and Universities

There are many colleges and universities in Ohio. Here are the more prominent, with their locations, dates of founding, and enrollments.

*Ashland College,* Ashland, 1878, 4,391

*Cy Young won more games (511) than any other major-league pitcher.*

*Baldwin-Wallace College,* Berea, 1845, 4,713

*Bowling Green State University,* Bowling Green, 1910, 18,043

*Capital University,* Columbus, 1850, 3,008

*Case Western Reserve University,* Cleveland, 1826, 8,386

*Central State University,* Wilberforce, 1887, 2,550

*Cleveland State University,* Cleveland, 1923, 18,534

*College of Mount St. Joseph,* Cincinnati, 1920, 2,566

*College of Wooster,* Wooster, 1866, 1,787

*The Defiance College,* Defiance, 1850, 1,006

*Denison University,* Granville, 1831, 2,027

*Heidelberg College,* Tiffin, 1850, 1,303

*Hiram College,* Hiram, 1850, 930

*John Carroll University,* Cleveland, 1886, 4,407

*Kent State University,* Kent, 1910, 23,727

*Kenyon College,* Gambier, 1824, 1,524

*Marietta College,* Marietta, 1835, 1,365

*Miami University,* Oxford, 1809, 16,157

*Mount Union College,* Alliance, 1846, 1,359

*Muskingum College,* New Concord, 1837, 1,122

*Notre Dame College of Ohio,* Cleveland, 1922, 827

*Oberlin College,* Oberlin, 1833, 2,920

*Ohio Northern University,* Ada, 1871, 2,595

*The Ohio State University,* Columbus, 1870, 52,895; Lima, 1960, 1,313; Mansfield, 1958, 1,336; Marion, 1957, 1,161; Newark, 1957, 1,582

*Ohio University,* Athens, 1804, 16,500; Belmont, St. Clairsville, 1957, 1,080; Chillicothe, 1946, 1,501; Ironton, 1956, 1,477; Lancaster, 1968, 1,369; Zanesville, 1946, 1,385

*Ohio Wesleyan University,* Delaware, 1842, 1,966

*Otterbein College,* Westerville, 1847, 2,315

*University of Akron,* Akron, 1870, 28,967

*University of Cincinnati,* Cincinnati, 1819, 30,737

*University of Dayton,* Dayton, 1850, 11,284

*University of Toledo,* Toledo, 1872, 23,926

*Ursuline College,* Cleveland, 1871, 1,526

*Wilberforce University,* Wilberforce, 1856, 779

*Wilmington College,* Wilmington, 1870, 890

*Wittenberg University,* Springfield, 1845, 2,340

*Wright State University,* Dayton, 1964, 17,423

*Xavier University,* Cincinnati, 1831, 6,477

*Youngstown State University,* Youngstown, 1908, 14,864

**Where To Get More Information**
Ohio Division of Travel and Tourism
30 East Broad Street
P.O. Box 1001
Columbus, OH 43266
Or Call 1-800-BUCKEYE

# Bibliography

## General

Aylesworth, Thomas G., and Virginia L. Aylesworth. *Let's Discover the States: Eastern Great Lakes*. New York: Chelsea House, 1988.

## Indiana

Aylesworth, Thomas G., and Virginia L. Aylesworth. *Indiana*. Greenwich, CT: Bison Books, 1985.

Carpenter, Allan. *Indiana*, rev. ed. Chicago: Childrens Press, 1979.

Dillion, Lowell I., and E. E. Lyon, eds. *Indiana: Crossroads of America*. Dubuque, IA: Kendall/Hunt, 1978.

Esarey, Logan. *A History of Indiana*. 2 vols. in one. Indianapolis: Hoosier Heritage Press, 1970.

Hoover, Dwight W., and Jane Rodman. *A Pictorial History of Indiana*. Bloomington: Indiana University Press, 1981.

Nolan, Jeanette. *Indiana*. New York: Coward, McCann & Geoghegan, 1969.

Peckham, Howard H. *Indiana: A Bicentennial History*. New York: Norton, 1978.

Wilson, William E. *Indiana: A History*. Bloomington: Indiana University Press, 1966.

## Michigan

Bailey, Bernadine. *Picture Book of Michigan*, rev. ed. Chicago: Whitman, 1967.

Carpenter, Allan. *Michigan*. rev. ed. Chicago: Childrens Press, 1978.

Catton, Bruce. *Michigan: A History*. New York: Norton, 1984.

Dunbar, Willis F. *Michigan: A History of the Wolverine State*, rev. ed. Grand Rapids, MI: Eerdman, 1980.

Fradin, Dennis B. *Michigan in Words and Pictures*. Chicago: Childrens Press, 1980.

## Ohio

Carpenter, Allan. *Ohio*, rev. ed. Chicago: Childrens Press, 1979.

Collins, William R. *Ohio: The Buckeye State*, 6th ed. Englewood Cliffs, NJ: Prentice Hall, 1980.

Crout, George C. , and W. E. Rosenfelt. *Ohio: Its People and Culture*. Minneapolis, MN: Denison, 1977.

Havinghurst, Walter. *Ohio: A Bicentennial History*. New York: Norton, 1976.

Renick, Marion L. *Ohio*. New York: Coward, McCann & Geoghegan, 1970.

Roseboom, Eugene H., and Francis P. Weisenburger. *A History of Ohio*. 2nd ed. Columbus: Ohio Historical Society, 1984.

## Photo Credits/Acknowledgments

Photos on pages 3 (top) and 5 courtesy of Indiana Historical Bureau; pages 6-7, 9, 10, 11, 13-16, 18, 19, and 22 courtesy of Indiana Dept. of Commerce; pages 3 (middle), 23-26, 28, 29, 31-33, 36, and 37 courtesy of Michigan Travel Bureau; pages 30 and 34 courtesy of Metropolitan Detroit Convention & Visitors Bureau; pages 38 (upper left) and 39 courtesy of the State Archives of Michigan; pages 3 (bottom) 41, 43, 45, 46, 48, 51, 53-57, and 59 courtesy of Ohio division of Travel & Tourism; pages 49 and 50 courtesy of Ohio Historical Society; pages 20, 21, and 58 (top) courtesy of New York Public Library Picture Collection; page 39 courtesy of Kellogg Company; pages 42-42 courtesy of Terry Cartwright, page 47 courtesy of Dave Giorgis, page 52 courtesy of David J. Castelli, page 58 (bottom) courtesy of New York City Ballet; Page 60 courtesy of the National Baseball Library.

Cover photograph courtesy of Michigan Travel Bureau.